Oooooo......!!!

To Whomever calls for
a Chat..... Well,

I have been up all night
~~trying~~ to grapple with
work (words) towards a
new "Collection" of
poems, which will simply
be entitled:
" Oooooo...." !.!.!

Please — please — please
leave me be, for a
DAYTIME ~~REST~~ & SLEEP
Period....

Thank you.

p.s. If urgent, leave a "Note"
~~tucked~~ under my door! ← Home →

Oooooo......!!!

Hone Tuwhare

STEELE ROBERTS
AOTEAROA NEW ZEALAND

© Hone Tuwhare 2005

Thanks to Glennis and Norman Woods of Kaka Point for
all sorts of things, not least gathering the material; to Sue
and Richard Hatherly for similarly marvellous support; to
Caroline Foote for editorial work; to Janet Hunt for literary
archaeology; to Zoë Gower and Tangaroa for the cover
photo; to Toby Bishop, Michele Clarke, Daisy Coles, Fiona
Glanville, Laura Ranger and Stephannie Tims for
production assistance; and Lynn Peck for cover design.

National Library of New Zealand
Cataloguing-in-Publication Data
Tuwhare, Hone, 1922-
Oooooo.....!!! / Hone Tuwhare.
ISBN 1-877338-69-9
I. Title.
NZ821.2—dc 22

Steele Roberts Ltd
Box 9321 Wellington Aotearoa New Zealand
phone 04 499 0044 • fax 04 499 0056
info@SteeleRoberts.co.nz • www.SteeleRoberts.co.nz

Contents

Mmmmmmm

I sing you a mini-waiata
I'm burbling it out like a tui.
Kia ora and kia kaha –
With my arohanui

Hone

Making easy-going words of magic

Lyric

I am buttoning up
    the buttons of my
    mouth: and now
    with only one to
    go — I'm whistling
    you a love-song
    of longing from
    the wilderness —
    — the throb & choke
    that may only
    come from the
    musical palette
    of my craven
    heart; hear —
    o, hear me!

And love my truth.

Meander, but trap the meaning of your thoughts, on paper

For reasons
    I cannot say
    nor state
    nor overcome a tendency
    vague, nor infer an abandoned modesty, to
    have them
    cast in stone? No.

No... no... no! And to you,
    Fate, a double, 'no-no' —
    which in Māori, means
        'arse-holes' (nono)
            to
            you,
      Fate! And to my
    hand, unfalteringly —

I say: Go! Go for it! Let
    your writing-wrist
    flex, curve lovingly, making easy-going words of magic
    — on the paper. Yea!

Some thoughts (*mad ones*)

In the 'Book of John' (Hone)
     that's to say, *MY book* —
or, books (I've had ten (10) pub-
lications, all told) one may say,
that I have been a prolific
writer/author — and — and, *still*
going, still cajoling, provocatively
the Muse, to keep the creative
doors, of mad/sophisticate &
ingenuous ideas, readily &
at hand, for me to reform,
or re-construct — re-model?

     Ah, well — what better
way to live one's Life, in
an objective & positive way
     of re-interpreting Life (!)
          as Hone (John) would
sense it, feel it, taste
     it & if it's flavourful,
          EAT IT?!!
          or,
Suckle and lick it (!)
     the feminine clitorial
          Temple of Sensuality
            and Love? O, YEA!

POEM! By me, Hone

I am drinking
    in the House
    Bar, of my
    favourite Watering
    Hole in Dunedin
    called, the
        'TANIWHA,'
    that is,
The LEVIATHAN!
    It is nearly mid-
    night or, 'early-
    pearly' Day, herald-
    ing, another day
    of a life I should
    not characterize
    as character-
    less, or even,
    banal. NEVER!!
        Because —
    poetry digs deeper
    under the skin,
        where
    the emotive force
    of creativity may
    only 'kick in', re-
    spond,
    when it is tickled
    persuasively, by
    yr own, co-operativ-
    ely, awakened MUSE,
    to dance, sing, even
    'do' the HAKA, War-
    dance, of joy & re-
    lease... yup!!!

Opportunely, rain?

Again, tonight I hear you rain, ironing-out the corrugations
   on my tin roof, my worried brow? I reckon, in sum, I'll
   survive the featured, non-eventium-Millennium, with
   only a paucity of glum. And, if mystic occurrences take
   place that are beyond my experience of them, then in
   concurrence, I should be obliged to fart heartily,
   if not, thunderously ... Oh, if could only refrain from
   sucking my wettened hitch-hike thumb, and pull all my
   fingers out of the veiny-vain-bloodiness, of my afflicted
   haemorrhoidal anus — then, and only then, will I rid me
   of that low-down feeling of defensiveness like, I'm up
   against, The Whole World? Moreover, a
   rumour-label is already pinned on me, "O, here's
   another opportunistic lout!" (sing it soft, not lout). And,
   I prefer much, the word, 'opportunely', to,
   'opportunistic'? Opportunely has a better
   melodic flow. It has more class — like, CLASS? Hey! I
   think I am getting more demure, obscure; subjective,
   here? A covert, cowering-down? A secretion of a
   deficiency pertaining to a more working-class militancy,
   of expression? Maybe, that is what ambiguity in poetry
   is all about. Why Critics work assiduously
   digging out the true meaning of a word, embedded in
   context (retaining within itself, a double/multiple
   meaning; flexibility) thereby disclosing the writer's
   social/class loyalties & clout. Finally, is sententiousness
   in art, forgivable, regrettable, forgettable? Hey, I'm on
   to it. Move over, or out ... (not to worry,
   ist mein Name, you see?)

'Wind stroked'

Wind stroked,
plucked;
the Power Lines, defer.
They're singing a song
of Power, deferred —
and are enviously
listening to the
light-hearted ditty —
(in a higher key)
thinly penetrative
& harmonically
repetitive;
Bugger Off!
Bugger Off!
Defensively, Power-lines
surge in reply, raising
the Voltage —
Ecstatically (!)
Your Power is of the Elements,
Wind —
But mine, is Man-Driven
and sourced from
River Power
Dam-med!

'In the Beginning: was, THE WORD'

In the Beginning: was, THE WORD. THE *only* one.
    And yet... I, I, I, am now under Siege
        by thousands of 'em (!)
        Stoically, I accept my
        FATE — dourly,
          rather poorly
        'Ah, well' — as Robbie
          Burns would say: 'just
          pass me that bottle, of Glenfiddich (!)'

But... words (?) Ah, Yes... WORDS — a personal
    Treasury of emotively-charged, meanings
    that means a lot to some — and *nothing*
        to others!
For me — a 'build up' of a rhythmically
    musical treasure-trove (AHEM!) to
    which I subject & apply cajolery, by
    stoking the fickle, freshly discovered
    forge, of my Māori Humour — together,
        with a modicum of that saucy
          element, known as *Creativity*!
        'Snot easy, Bros...

    And, and — WOT of my seizmic mentality
    and frustrations?! Groping, groping in the
    dark, for the politer, Upper Class meaning
    for the 'piggy-back', word for '*Rooting*'?
        (for, fuck-sake)!

        When,
          in
        anycase
        THAT, WORD
        juice-extracted,
          dry —

is no longer in abundance,
but, may be sought
instead —
doin'
a Boogie-Woogie whirl,
and twirl, like: letting
your Partner out at full arms' length,
and bringin' her home again —
close (Oh, so very close) breast,
to, 'Beastie Breast!' murmuring;
murmuring, tenderly, the Worlds' best
lie (second only to 'Bill' Shakespeare's
puling & quality rantings) — and,
murmuring, murmuring over & over again — again,
O, just 'clichély' boring — boring — and without pause
— forging each golden syllable; exotic Māori phrasing,
as I sit in a, Classic Phylosophic state of deep
contemplation, on my wooden lavatory-bowl Seat,
— where *ALL* great concepts, poetically inventive
& conjured-up, and timed to a tick-tocking
second, to emerge together — with each
sloppy, floppy, phylosophical PLOP!

'The pen writes'

The pen writes; the penis
    waits — and all movement
    is — in suspension until
    the women send forth their
    best if not a more arrogant
    voice among them to call
    the men, their women & daughters,
    to meal — but, *not* before
    a group-ritual song of welcome
    is in accord with the
    invitational & gay, light-heartedness
    temper & gait of the welcoming
    action-song to come & join
    the affray together, of the
    sharing & the breaking of the
    bread of love.

My mind meanders, because I hate to shift my Māori arse to concoct a menu, *à la Māori*

My mouth is roofless, & bereft
of the Cud, of Creative
Ideas — to move things (or,
me) — along
more positive pathways to
those elusive goals
that always seem
attainable — but have never
succumbed to my written
prayers that are
insincerely
beggarlie & at times,
auspiciously
without form, or merit.
O, Mistress Muse — why
oh why are you
so elusive?

Well,
there is nothing going on, in my defeatist
frustrative Mind, that is taking the punches
of Truth — above, & below my jaw, my
belly-button 'PITO' (which is, at present,
in vast complaint) and, methink, the only
Solution is to have a favourite, 'boil-up'
of PŪHĀ, PORK-BONES &
DUMPLINGS. O... YEA!

Janet Paul

(A Dame? But — but —
 I had always known you
 were THE ONE. THE ONE!)

I missed the Cross-over — and
 very much so, when — five long
 months afterwards, I gleaned, at last
 from the discovery — of an old surplus rag
 put aside on top of a heap of them — to light
 my wood-fire stove — that *you'd* gone!

Gone! Gone — gone, to the Gonna-land
 where everyone — each in their
 due-time, subsides — and is
 finally joined with the greatest
 dam (DAME (?)) *of all* —
 'Mummie' EARTH —
 our *Dearest*, Mother!

JANET PAUL (A Dame?
 Well … I had always known YOU …
 were THE ONE) — my first
 Publisher (1964) Hell,
 would you believe it?! Forty
 years ago?

Kereihi

Shirley Grace ('Kereihi') & Hone Tuwhare
JOHN MILLER PHOTO

**thin pome
for S.G.
from
me**

the
long-stemmed
daffodils
you thrust
at me
suddenly

now
are showing
off
not gloomily
stroppily
or yellowly
but sunnily —

their
green economy
of line
reminds me
of you
disrobed —
perhaps —
waiting in your
bed
for me
to
arrive!

I
would come
if I could
not
gloomily
not
fussily
maybe
sloppily
certainly
happily,
any way.

Kereihi ('Standing quite still')

Standing quite still we stare out
    over the City through the upstairs windows
    of your townhouse: we were twin spoons, back
    to front, or, just lumped together under
    a stretched jersey buttoned up.

Over your left shoulder my eyes traced
the forgotten lineaments of Rangitoto, the white
harbour lying somnolent in the moonlight.

But my eyes are second guessing:
    they're withdrawn. It's the memory of clearer
    sightings of you and the City that is pushing
    the moonbeams aside…
    You have Presence, élan. Townhouse, and now
    here … at Tomarata, where the stars at night
    bully and make swollen the ocean — and me meek.

You're all around me — matt bordered
framed or unframed, the pictures on canvas,
on paper, staring out of the walls give an
exuberant feel of people, cats, cars, a huge
sword that would take two hands to wield, the
slender arms of the harbour drenched with
colour, beckoning … Well, I love the

unostentatious, rough-sawn roofbeams of your house;
exposed, unabashed, and under which I have snored
and snored without causing any structural damage.
…At risk of being presumptuous, it must be said:
and I say it

because it seems absolutely right to retain
the smallest hope that you too may remember the sun
and sum of my embraces, without ever knowing that
there were times when memories such, bestow a thin
moon of wretchedness — an abyssmal affliction
of torment of emptiness — to my arms to my hands
to my lips: Kereihi

To safe harbour & estuary come

Swallow, swallow
 are you memory-driven to return
 over such vast distances to the mud-nests

 you've built and stuck like mounds
 of plaster to the sheltered walls
 of my porch & barn?

Doorless and windowless
 should the boards of my house one day
 lie flat on the ground staring sightlessly

 at the sky, will history record that two
 houses once — yours and mine — snuggled
 up together for warmth?

Leave Capistrano and the harsh face
 of a northern winter. My hope is as big
 as the gulp of my heart for your returning.

O, come back quickly, swallow — quickly
 to Pakiri.

Like, it's personal?

Maybe it was the low seductive caress of a melody
    in a minor key played by the flautist at that
    tea-shop on the Peninsula?

Or perhaps it was some kind of fish-bone or trip-wire
    catching me in the throat in a sort of mid-reverie
    blues as the sky drew on some dark second-hand
    clothes fraying badly at the edges — and the rain
    bouncing merrily off the concrete?
    Whatever.

I began to reconstruct a song that was once an unvoiced
    blues reverie (my eyes are a give-away, I wished
    my face a blotter) articulating each word carefully
    with an exaggeration that made my friends shuffle
    and cough forgiving me, but turning away, vowing:
    T'hell with it, pure corn — he can't sing.

It's been two hours gone since my throat got tripped up on
    the fish-bone-wire in there. I feel a lot better after
    several cups of strong tea sugar and full-creamed milk
    with a dunked dog-biscuit or two inside me. But what
    was it exactly?

The ground is damp and steaming and the sky naked
    in its blueness, with the sun exposing itself and
    pissing cancer down on everybody spread out and awake
    and over half-way round the world ball? Terrific.

I see heat-shimmer rising from the tarseal.

The backbone of things

I look skew-whiff at the way
    you shape your feelings through
    your fingers, your brushes;
    the angular swish of arms
    and hips as you address
    the canvas — your eye
    checking the plumb-line for
    the lie of the face or of
    the land, with your hand
    held out at arm's length
    like a slim axe and
    I wonder what next as
    I sit for you eyes akimbo
    my arms held stiffly down
    my sides, my piles begin-
    ning to give me arseholes.

    and I think, oh boy, thus
    far for me & no further:
    then you lay your brushes
    down and you invite me
    to have a look. I look.

It is a dark summary of all
    my joyful sins and I
    don't say nothing for a minute:

    maybe we could proscribe
    each other by placing
    the result of each one's
    recent *ouvrage* side by side
    to make a two-pager —
    a tiny book together —
    a love story full of storm
    and tears — full of storm
    and tears and love —
    but mostly love. Always

Humming

It is a house to be constructed with care
    for it has no confining walls
    thus permitting expansion: vertical

    growth is not inhibited for there
    is no limit to the height of the ceiling
    stretching to heaven. This house
    can endure given a chance, that's
    for sure ... H m m m m

But since it is of earth its foundations may be
    built of sand: and because there are
    no confining walls this fragile house
    of love may be seen as layers of light
    and colour — a feeling tone — warm, purple
    orange grey hot and cold with lots of blue
    and yellow to make it green — green
    and predictable ... H m m m m

Fleshed out though, this house of love isn't
    ageless, but ages old. It has form; contour.
    It has presence; a brilliant arc uniting
    heaven and hell; love-thoughts in pursuit of
    a physical expression — a noisy, gloppy
    proclamation —

        Aha   Aha — Aha — Aha   Aha

... and horses, huffing and pounding into
the straight, riders snarling, cruel whips
flailing — the anguish of stretched leather
reeking sweetly of sweat ... And reason? Ahh.

Reason is a hunchback of irrelevance backing
quietly out the door.

But where are the flowers — the select flowers
    of endearment, soul-food to dazzle the heart?

    O, they're here, all right: there, there
    and THERE ... H m m m m

I dream of the erotic, not of oppression — but release

He: You are not a no-account. For I share a delight, but am not accountable for those qualities in you, that are beautiful, and remarkable.

She: No other woman can have that part of you that is me. You, therefore, are the sum of me. It is not a decree or holy writ but a truth re-written — not yesterday, or even one hour ago, but a sacred truth born just now — and presently, crying lustily for attention: attend to it without words: mouth me!

He: I kiss your eyes — which are those of a wild animal. Your mouth I press and stop up with mine — lest more riches — the sacred oils of extravagance — escape, and are lost in the anonymity of the vast night air — the moon's curved mouth, laughing.

She: My darling, the night, the hour, the moment — can never slake their thirst enough, at my inexhaustible spring — my treasury of the fleshly lore of the senses — my love and lust for you, my darling man.

He: My lover, my heart — my three-fold, infolded, and secret lips of pleasure — in thee I drown to the pulsating drum — to the piercing waters of joy and pleasure — and the loss: I am drowning, I drown, and inside you I get on with it; swimming.

Caretaker's report from Tomarata Estate

I should like to report that the pines are swaying elegantly
on long black legs; their spiny heads soughing in the
breeze. But they're not. Instead, their heads twitch
impatiently away from each other in a heated animated
discourse — especially the group on the skyline to the
right of the 'Workshop'. They're talking past each
other in loud voices. I've never been so distracted. It's
like nurturing a minority terrorist group in the
classroom. If you like, I could walk rings around the
ring leaders tomorrow — and threaten them with a
chainsaw. I'm being extravagant. Forgive me for the
underlying note of petulance: it's the wind you know?
The wind — in the afternoon? And now —

The wind is flattening the long pasture grasses exposing
their light undersides with a magic hair brush,
enhancing the seemingly endless hypnotic snake-like
movement of flow and ebb, of sunlight and shadow.

Withered leaves dislodged by the wind from a mossy
peach tree growing right on the edge of the verandah,
flash past me horizontally, like darts. I watch from a
sheltered niche at the eastern end of the verandah my
elbows high on the table, my hands nursing a coffee
mug of tea enriched with milk and honey. I face first
this way and that on the swivel chair like a film
director, plantation owner, train driver. I feel
important. On the settee beside me your faithful
guard-cat Barry, is resting coiled and relaxed, his
responsibilities shared; his daily supply of victuals
assured. I'm spoiling him: he's the guardian spirit of
the place, that's why. He's treating me now with the
colossal indifference of the privileged — and the fat-
puku(ed).

I am learning to keep still and have insinuated a naked foot
out of the verandah shade to test the sun's heat. I can
feel it now, because the force of the wind has abated.

A variety of birds, multi-coloured, have acquired a
phony imperturbable air of, "I don't give a shit,
mate, but that worm and that crust of bread you've
chucked on the lawn, is MINE!" Well, the pecking
order is determined by size, which is flexible.
Victory goes to the quickest and the hungriest. The
only animals around are Barry and me, and a white
horse grazing near another fine stand of pines
artfully spaced to let hurricane winds go through
without impediment. Dogs are not conspicuous
except where they're exorcised on the beach. Which
may be a pity. For the banded dotterel — which
makes itself at home on the sand-dunes, are the
most caring little creatures; brave, too.

But absolutely dotty. If you go up to them for a closer
inspection and a chat, they run off together about
ten feet, then stop. No, they've never used their
wings in panic. You try a more cautious and
diplomatic approach and they run off again — little
tiny feet churning up the sand. The direction
they've chosen to run off to appears to be randomly
chosen and when you approach them again they
split; run off for another ten feet in opposite
directions where they both looked back at us (but
that was way back when) to see if we're both
following the play. Well, I can't say I am. I choose
the wee one who's gone to the left — because the
sand's firmer and it's beginning to dawn on me that
this could go on for ever. You choose to come with
me because you know how I hate scrambling over
shifting sand: hateful stuff (I've actually built better
castles out of the substantial variety and materials of
the mind *) To our surprise, the other dotty bird's
been following us. It's only five feet away. We
extend a placatory hand to it and shuffle back   31
towards it. It powers away on its tiny feet in a

different direction, then stops only seven feet away.
FUCK IT. That's it. I break off a piece of outjutting
sandstone to chuck at it — and the other begins twitting
me about my fuckn manners. We're actually closer now
to the homestead. I want a cup of tea I mutter walking off
aloofly, fuckm. You stick an arm through mine: they're
only luring us away from their nests, I think. O, do you
think so? I say. Let's look them up in your bird book,
then; identify them absolutely.

I look back. They're gone: their cheers and jeers like twitter-
ing bands of broken sunlight on our backs; warm though.

* *"It is enough that our fathers believed. They have exhausted the
faith-faculty of the species. Their legacy to us is the scepticism of
which they were afraid. ... the mystic leads us astray. ... for,
just as Nature is matter struggling into mind, so Art is mind
expressing itself under the conditions of matter, and thus, even
in the lowliest of her manifestations, she speaks to both sense
and soul alike. To the aesthetic temperament the vague is
always repellent."*

Kereihi, the quotation above is not by Karl Marx, who
has expressed himself on art, too, but by Oscar (Fingall
O'Flahertie Wills) Wilde. I was a bit surprised when you
told me you were attending, Seances. I hope I'm not
being pompous, or unreal. I think it's normal and human
to absorb pain at a quarter level; chucking away the
repetitive mental ones. But being obsessively in love with
one person is a disaster! I have to pick up some things at
Uni. today (Tuesday? It's 12:25am!) Good morning —
and love. I must hit the sack to be able to catch the rare
'millionaire bus' down Island Bay Road at 9:45am. It
comes back at 5:55pm, leaving town; the only one down
this way. Handy. Sorry about the flamboyant envelope.

Trietise?

It's good to be
permanently
disemployed —
so
that my longing
for you
is in no way
a disfigured form
of our love
for each other,
but an architecturally
melding
of our flesh
breathlessly
inspired, and twinly
conspired
in an angelic
form of flesh
& pounding
blood, in no
way, dishonoured,
but achieving
for the Zenith of power
of ONE (enjoined)
… where the victory of one, over the other, is
never a game of Solitaire — but
of one flesh, companionably loving, heartfelt,
& for that moment … forever.

To: the death of a former lover —
whose tangihanga I could *not* attend

for 'Tieeri' — whose body, lying in state,
at her tangihanga at Pakiri — took place —
in my absence. She would know why.

And I (?) Well ...
I am bleeding
copiously —
like a continual
heavy downpour
of rain
And ... and, as
far as I can
make out —
the 'Sky-piss'
& its relieving
(— relieving?)
down-flow
bear no relation-
ship to my
tears
for you ... YOU,
who have gone,
gone, gone — leaving
me, utterly bereft ...

Gimme — O, gimme!

(A living verse) A 'Life-source', indeedy!

The cuisine, rural, countrified,
   is comprised of delicious
   bounty that only the Good
   Earth, with motherly grace —
   can permit a favoured son
   to take, partake, inchoate (?)
   cook-up, or, their rawness
   (e.g. raw fish-flesh), sprinkled
   in a Holy Sense of seizure
   (seizure?) and an un-
   tabled manner, gulped, sans
   plate fork or knife, and
   with holiness, using thumb
   and fore-finger-rub, sprinkle
   salt, lemon-juice, from
   a halved-lemon, — and
   O, o, oh! Dear Me: go,
   go, go-for-it! Fill the un-
   patient body, with Nature's
   gifts. O, yummy!
      (at my humble abode
         in South Otago, by
         Tangaroa's friendly
         side. Yup...)!!!

'Just at this moment'

Just
at this moment in Time,
I'm not at all
inspired
to put down words
of rhythmic strain
together, with those other
more relaxed elements
of mystical flavour to
knock my hip-bone —
knee-bone & foot to
a Haka Beat, un-asham-
edly borrowed from
the Tango Dance —
steps & Jazz, rather
hesitant with regard to
the former (the Tango)
& the more on-going
four/four beat, of Jazz.
Gimme — O, gimme!

Yes! Pack it into me, Man!
Louis Armstrong, Gene Krupa
Artie Shaw, & that crooning
Low-down up-beat of Trombone
Player: ME? (so, sorry!)

Blow that horn, man

And ... and ... and —
permission
may not be
granted, for admission
to that Holy Temple
of Femininity
whereto the Player's
lips are applied,
whereon, some skill
on, 'Horn-
blowing', is unmistakably
required, specifically,
in that feminine
area where
a certain expertise —
in an 'Introductory
sense', &, aptly
named
in the Musical
Accord of a
heightened sense —
whereon the 'Biblical
Character, called,
Job' — may be aptly
recalled (in a more
'Modernistic Sense!')
as
'The Blow Job!'
Ooooo!!!

PS A high-step, low-step, Ball-room & Jive-like jingle,
   dedicated to Russell, Meg & Katie, for the
   ATTRACTIVE XMAS CAROL TO ME OF
   WARM Greetings.

Dilemma

Do not doubt me
if I am enslaved by
the wiggle and prance
of your body's gestures —
your preenings, the way
the light escapes when
you throw your hair
back from your brow;
the articulate fluency
of eye & lip that insist
I need not be
enslaved, but step out
free at once of encumbrances
that have become as
heavy as chains. I should
love you more if you
were to go, she said.
How can I explain?
Must I doubt the evidence
of my senses & heart?
Must I now believe that
the skies are not engorged
with stars, the sea-lanes windless
and slack & truth is love turned
into a pitiless lie?
Must I go?

Tangaroa (betcha)

I'm entranced. Forever
   by the wiggle-twiggle
   of the feminine poetry
   you, my dear, communicate
   to a charmed World... YES!
      WORLD? er... um...
      Let me qualify this —
   My World! (selfishly) *My World*!

And when you does your attractive
   eye-locking imprisonment of
   my (normally) disinterested
   eye-ing of anything other
   than food (mutton-birds, *Tī-tii*,
      e.g. are the end! — the paradisical
   end of *all* the heavenly tastes
   that OUR *good* & *kind* Gods
      (*MĀORI* ones)!
Are pleased to ration out
      to the deserving! *So*, I must
      behave & pay my proper
   respects & ancient prayers
      (NOT PĀKEHĀ ones)!
to Rangi, Papa, Rongo,
   Tūmatauenga & not
      the least, TANGAROA!! Gotcha!

Is this jazz we're talkin' abt?

They're not exertive, nor anything like,
    sportive, Beach Girls & Boys —
    hoping to acquire the benefits
    of an orange-coloured tan
    on pale bodies, legs & arms!!! No way.

I am secretly amused as mine genes
    have established a
    Monopoly of Tannery Factories, to
    assure that a skin-colour,
    'drift-off', will never be a threat!

And, by Nature's perverse contrivances,
    blandly — *à la Humoresque* (!) —
    stylishly, underplayed, &
    covertly so, and together with the expressive
    pitch of Louis Armstrong's Horn,
    the soothing uplift of a Coleman
    Hawkins' Saxophone — the gentle
    'washing' of sounds, stylistically
    unadorned, by Gene Krupa's
    artistic flourishes, to give
    the Soloists, time, and room —
    for freedom, freedom, freedom
    of Movement!!! O! Yea!!!
    ALL, to: four beats to a bar??
      IMPOSSIBLE!!!!
    But — but — but, artistic
    soloists & Jazz Wizardry
    — *without loss of individuality*,
    CAN, make it happen…
        and…
      it happens!!!! O,
        yes, indeedy!

Kina!

Hey-ho! My pine-needling
    Oceanic Cuzzie —
        you — yes!
        you —

nestling there, elusively —
    and trying to look
        unpalatably, un-attractive

Not a chance!
    Better, to do
a re-count of your needle
    points, Chum ... because,

your last days shall be over-
        whelmed by the smug
    glimmer-shimmer of the
    'Tai-aha like,' pokie-wokie
    glisten of my soupie-slurpful
throttle, as I expertly balance —
        with artistic delicacy,
your needle-point-like
        movements —
in the loving palms of my
        Māori hands!
I do not forget to sing a Tapu Hymn
        of, THANK YOU —
to our Sea God, TANGAROA
for its Life-giving, and — and,
much-prized bounties
    from its sea-chest of alternate
        varieties, like, pipi, tuangi, toheroa,
           tio, kina, together with the sea-going fish, with
        the hula-hips & wiggles, and
           sparkling jewellery, to match
             the choicest — like, BIG, seductive eyes

        O! YEA!

Thelonius Monk in 'A' flat?

I'm hooked right into you, my dear, my love —
    and when your saucy quips
    incite me to caress your hips
    I cannot stop you, when you
    whirl into a dance, that's not
    at all extravagant or showy, and,
    least of all, rock-steady and
    immovable. But, with a minimalist
    paucity of movement of the breasts —
    or, cheeky globular whorl
    and tightening of the wonderful
    cheeks of a shapely arse!

I think, quite firmly (it's my belief)
    that the element of candour and
    of provocation, stirs the male
    and malefunctionary parts of me
    to urgent life, upstartingly! And well …

Musically, it may be usefully compared —
    to a rhythmic-jump-stonk-plonk
    of a chordic introspective
    clutch and ripple of one — maybe
    two, handfuls of the black and white
    piano keys. Yeah! Like, so, man!
    Thelonius Monk? Signing off! GOTCHA!

A paean of praise for the succulent bounty from our Sea-God, Tangaroa (*I repeat: raw*)

The Sun has gone on — without surcease —
    to put a shine on other regions —
    (geographically speaking) as the World —
    our World — spins, lop-sidedly in
    space — first baring the left hand
    cheek of its arse; then, the right side.

I can't get used to these independent
    'show-offness'… and so — will
    desist & not give a damn no more
    till what they call Moon Day or,
    Doomsday, or, something more familiar
    like, Sun Day — Picnic Day, at the
    Cockle-Spitting Contest — when the
    Mussels can't be cajoled into turning
    a hairy hair and the internal
    wee wick of its Clitorae quivers with glee!

Well, with a pair of small scissors, I snip
    and de-hair the Clitorae — and,
    and… and, the limpid & raw
    & succulent flesh of the mussels
    invites me to rush in, open-mouthed,
        to partake in a banquet
            of *raw*, fleshly delight…
                O! Yea!!! Very Sexy!!!

Shopping list,
melodically askance, & yet, *bombed*

Right up there, on high, *Te Atua*
    commands the rainbow god,
    Aniwa-niwa, to envelop the
    rivers, the mountains & valleys
    with its admirable mantle of
    many colours, knowing ere-long,
    jealousy & envy, are the
    natural colours sought by
    wind, rain, sun-bursts ...

My heart lifts — is enlightened
    thus, as I lean down to
    kiss you, discerning, that
    you too are similarly en-
    tranced by the infectious
    way in which Nature beckons
    to Mankind with the magic
    command, unheralded by
    the sweet sounds of strings
    plucked, honked — or
    melodically sawn to their
    heightened pitch — ending
    with the lisping notes
    denoting a memorable
    human inventiveness,
    succinctly appropriate: holy ...

Jive

As the music heats up
    and the four beats to
    the bar are more insistently
    emphatic, I go into
    a captive trance that is
    not at all immobile, stilly —
    or even silly. Rather
    more like a stylish swing &
    jive sort, of boogie-woogie
    prance? Me adam's apple,

    in a slide-trombonic glide, is
    vertically a-quiver, and,
    as me rubbled voice in song
    contributes — not untunefully —
    to the joyful holy farce,

    it is in matchless co-ordination with the wibble-
    wobble swerve
    and wiggle-swivel
    of me rhythmic Māori arse.

Ode to a blowfly

I see you maggot,
cuddled around
a spear of grass
growing from a mere
jumble of now-fleshless
bones — the left-overs
of a sumptuous feast. Soon
your body will change
your wings glisten &
dry, and as you
draw strength from
the Sun; check the
pads on your feet
take flight & buzz
the odours of a rich
man's kitchen or the
weeping sores of the
poor. Your nose has
identified the strength
& density of smell
of each target. The
wild uncontrolled sound
of your buzzing indicates
how maddening it is
to make a choice.

It is also a signal to your kin
to shake off the blind torpors of the maggot-life,
for a life-style defying gravity & with
padded feet crawl over and around carrion
flesh savouring their taste & smell with infinite
    delicacy, leisurely, again, again, you wipe
  your feet on food before it reaches a human mouth.

'overnight'

overnight, the lone
    sausage, with
    only a slight
    kink to its back,
    stood as steadfast
    as a rock-cod,
    turned to stone …

The tentative jab
    of a three-pronged fork
    was twisted aside: splayed —
    a bowie-knife bluntened —
    a flowered design on a dish
      deflowered

Just thinkin', & dreaming

I cannot cajole
 the threatening herd
 of clouds
 in the sky, to
  'back-off', nor
 the rising insanities
  of wind-whirls, &
 an up-beat song
  of blues-tainted

morning-moanings,
  rising
 from my gravel-ly
  Māori throttle —
 just like a blues
  song & comedic
 solo, by my favourite
 interpretive vocalist
  horn-blower — Louis
 Armstrong!!! O, yea!!! *Bring it on*
 LOUIS... Bring
  it on, Man!

Karakia

If I should succumb
    to your voracious, green-eyed-
    depths, Tangaroa, then
    let it be so... for
    all beginnings have their
    source in you — in despite

    of all other human 'make-shift
    ones', calculated to appease
    other heavens of dubious
    qualities, except, the uncanny
    one (the best of all expletives)
    Get thee, 'fooked-up' & to
    hell — on your four-wheeled
    Charger: go ... *Aber*,
    GO!... GO!... GO! go well...
        Yea!

WOT!!! Not enough to go around?

*(Ahhh… we will a 'brake'
on our gluttony.)*

Tribal Wars between Coastal
   and Inland Tribes, were
   sparked by an arrogant
   assumption by the latter,
   that they had every right
   to access the edibly tasteful
   bounties, of the Sea God,
      TANGAROA …… But
… and but —
      since
that particular — rich in
the variety of Kina, Kūtai,
Tuangi/Pipi … and — and,
'Karahu' (that look like the
most-savoured/flavoured/
succulent sea-food, that
Tangaroa has on offer …)
     Well…
can I say more. Ah…
     Yes!
A *'Karakia'* of heartfelt
   Aroha, & Thank You,
     simply,
   to our Sea God,
    'TANGAROA'
   for its generosity —
     goodwill —
   offer of its
    Life-giving tasteful fare —
      simply — to keep me in a
    joyous Step & Dance —
       Oooooo!!!

As my hunger dictates

When I dream —
At any time of the day
Or night — I am not aware, that …
Dream-clouds, do not
obscure, the Holy Magical
Work — of that great
Architect — who requires
no Drawing-table, or
Blue-print, to reconstruct
newly, & with artistic aplomb,
the newness & neatness
of line, or, curvature
enwrapping my 'infant-nappie', &
voracious — cries, that are
already overful-filled — and are
calculated to deafen your ear drums!

The Earth-Mum's udders, are about
to be re-plenished! In the meantime, they are
hanging slackly, whilst
Our Earth-Mum, takes a break — &,
and a refill? and I?
I awake, with an eager thump — or
thumps, as my feet hit the floor — one, two! In this
respect, I shall be frank
with you …
      I am Hungry (!)
      ………………
      ………………

Mmmmmmm

'And in the moonlight'

And in the moonlight
I counted them and
there were nine rocks like smooth fingers
sticking out and three shining pools
which didn't seem to want to go
anywhere — and beyond, their quiet
domain, the river gushing by trying
to lower itself to just below my
height at its deepest point
so that I could stand &
still keep my head above
water, thoroughly
immersed; trapped by
your long scissoring legs
my mouth a junction
of hair and pubic mound
and you gurgling on your
flotative back, nearly drowning
in your joy and just then everything
stopped and I could
hear nothing any more
except the shrill calls
of crickets telephoning each
other up — suddenly we were treading
water & you were sitting on it hard
down and I could count only eight
rocks and the moon shat on us
brokenly and millions of crickets
thrilled and thrilled us as I bounded
up out of the bed of the river with
your thighs and legs enwrapped
about my hips like a rosary as you
began counting solemnly
in my deaf ear
leaving me breathless with wonder

Erotical feelings

Before you can lie (or lay) with woman
    you have to charm her by being
    lavishly over-complimentary
    about her womanly seductiveness
    so that you may have an
    easier physical access
    to the gleaming succulences
    that is her twig-gingly twigged
    clitorae (more obtrusive, now) —
    the alerted guardian, of the vertical,
    hair-adorned curvature, of her
    vaginal opening — to which I should
    like to introduce the veiny-vain
    musculature, that is my knob-headed
    penis rearin' & rarin' to push!
        Shove!! GO!! GO!!

p.s. Gawd!

Mmmmmmm, for the millennium

I will
come, if
you will me
to come. Cum,
you say? Oh!

Happy squeezings
then — and
pokings, easeful...
Mmmmmm...

Mary's song
(Wow! Jesus, I've cummed …!!!)

Alternate Title: Thank you, Jim. Now, one more
go. Mmmm … Loverly! You can go, now. Tell
no one. Bugger Off!

Knowing that Joseph was
incapable, to any extent,
of the positive act
of creation, the merriest
of all Marys, turned in-
stead to a sexy, robust
gent, called James (whom
she nick-named, Jim)
co-habiting with him
one fine day in April, with
great zest & fervour, & with
both, conjointly slipping
their bolts, clicketty-
clop, sloppity-slop, &
as near enough to the
joyous sound of church-
bells ringing out a
joyous hymnal in a
rocking & weaving
rumba-beat of marked
hesitancy & swerve; hip-
locked, limbs athwart —
to the holy sounds of Sun,
Wind & Ocean — applauding!

'Times like this, you have to excercise your affability!'

Thighs
rhymes with
sighs, especially
if they're intertwined
in movement holy,
wholly ... er, holey?!

Well, um ... on the
other hand, I shouldn't
think I'd "nod-off" in
the satiety of lustful
completion — if, suddenly,
you stuck a 'lustful'
pink & long-nailed finger
up my ring & quickly, &
in a torrent of self-
justification, coo honey-like,
in my ear : ... You're the risen
Christ! You are coming
sportively, sportively.. O!
— and very, very beautifully —
...... my darling, man (?)

O, shit! OUCH !!!

H. J.

fast POST
PAR AVION

Times like this, you have to exercise your affability!

Thighs
    rhymes with
    sighs, especially
    if they're intertwined
    in movement holy,
    wholly ... er, holey?!
    Well, um ... on the
    other hand, I shouldn't
    think I'd nod-off in
    the satiety of lustful
    completion —
    if, suddenly,
    you stuck a hurtful
    pink & long-nailed finger
    up my ring & quickly, &
    in a torrent of self-
    justification, coo honey-like,
    in my ear: ... *You're* the risen
    Christ! *You* are coming
    sportively, spurtively . . O!
    — and very, very beautifully —
    . . . . . my darling, man (!)
    O, shit! *OUCH!!!*

'Mark one up — for Miriam!

There's nothing going
on, (of what I
can view at night —)
on the surface
of the Moon — I mean...
No one has left
his signature on it,
to display the love &
aroha — of the pioneer
voyager — for his true
love, back on Earth —
where, ironically, his
"true love," is cradling
the body of another.
man, & moreover, with
~~a~~ true gusto & enthu-
siasm of a lover/woman
is sucking the rigid
penis of her new man — only
to see his noble stem
toppling, to her prof-
essional, "Axe-man -
Womans'-ship!" Ooooo...
"Up the Score — by One"!"
— for the Female Gender!..

#.T.

Secondary Title : Woman! Oh, yes! The central
& controlling Factor, in Humanity?
appending of Knowledge & scientific
"Peek-a-boo"! minutely! Tested -
Tested; Proven !!!! O, Yea!

... around me
are ideas; dreams-
a-whirling
... ...

Mark one up — for Miriam!

(Secondary Title: *Women!* Ah, yes! The central
& controlling factor, in Humanity's
expanding knowledge & scientific
'Peek-a-boo', minutely *tasted* —
tasted; proven!!!! O, Yea!)

There's nothing going
on (of what I
can view at night —)
on the surface
of the Moon — I mean...
No One has left
his signature on it,
to display the love &
aroha — of the pioneer
voyager — for his true
love, back on Earth —
where, ironically, his
'true love', is cradling
the body of another
man, & moreover, with
true gusto & enthu-
siasm of a lover/woman
is sucking the rigid
penis of her new man — only
to see his noble stem
toppling, to her prof-
essional, 'Axe-man-
Woman's-ship!' Ooooo...
'Up the Score — by *One*'
— for the Female Gender!!!

...around me
are ideas;
dreams —
aswirling

Just a thought

& if there are lovers
    I've forgotten, but
    not forgiven, then
    I chance, myself
    to be begotten to
    no one else
    but, of myself —
    forbidden & moreover
    forgotten … until

such moment in, Time? Well, & well —
    when all the ghosts
    of former lovers rise
    up to stab & stab
    taloned fingers, accusative —
    of the good times
    you've enjoined with
    them & in joyous
    movement of prodding
    gasped your last, O,
    your final gasp
    of expiration —
    satiation … O! & O! O!

Haiku-kuu

On my risen arse, deflating
your naked heels digging
me to go deeper — deeper.
Mmmmm ...... e e e e — yes

The pome that went astray!

(for F. — a Lady, 'unshowy' — and
    mannerly, tempered by that
    is not beggarly — but,
    rationally, in ample
    possession, her
    own precious store
    of that warm human stock
    that is called: humility...

But, I go on...! Because, I must.
    Your writings (in French) would
    baffle me — if it were not for
    the thoughtful fact — that you've
    deemed it a duty to supply me
    with a delightful translation
    in English — of the text,
    in French.

In Deutsch, I say to you, succinctly,
    "Danke Schön, meine Gnädige Frau.
    Sie, und thee ist Wunderbar! Aber..."

You pen a verse for me, to say (with just
    a trace of banality) that — "Spring is
    here ... etc" when everything, rising
    from the warm blanket of our great
    Earth Mum, is so greenly self-evident,
    which makes me put the brakes on my
    enthused wish to go rampant on you
    in a colourful, if not, Lyrical sense of
    a wave-like note, in suspension, &
    just within my musical grasp, calculated
    (naturally) to make you sit up and
    wonder how an old man of 82 years
    of age, can manage to lend some
    drama to notes released & climbing
    aloft & like a lasso twirling, embracing
    — circularly & together! But ...

Whii-ona

To a Lady-love, from
Timaru who may as well be
as far, far away as Timbuctoo!!!
And, and in true Kiwian accents, echo:
too bloody true, Mate!
... and, in a mournful
breath-heaving sigh of frustration — with the true
adhesion of thought, wonder, whether I shall ever
dine once more at your Holy
Temple of Sensuality,
Wonder & Joy. For me, a challenge
to that pink Clitorial Guardian
which, in a small, elegant series
of: Oh! O! O! OH! Spur me on to
cajole my veinie/vain
column of flesh, the arched
curvature of my voracious reptilian lick-lick
tongue to a
more human effort
Supremo! My Lady — love —
may we meet again? ... Come back ... Come.
YOU, my Dear, with your Regal
Visit, have blessed & paid honour
to my humble
abode
&
to me
Bless you, my Dear Lady, my ecstatic Joy & Longing
memorably, shall abide. How may it
be exceeded? I Love Thee...

How now knowest I, then?
I don't now know wot: nuffink?

On rare occasion, when good fortune
shines a light on me, I'm enamoured by the owner
of a plummy voice, "eye — see-aay" (I say) rich;
and full of deferred promise. To my

inquiry — not the least encumbered by indirect hints —
"Well, wot's yr fucking price?"
"O", she breathed, eye-balls flashing whitely, "No mood
I'm in, to indulge your brown biscuity-needs, today, thank
you" — and with that, an edgie-cornered stone (plum-
enjuiced) fell out of her mouth — and which I caught
with a swooping dexterity, just (gently brushing the
mound of her belly) — close to the cobbled, in-twisted
navel of her, and — "O", she cried, her eyes spark-
ling, "I've never seen such keen, anticipatory reaction!"
"I can do better," I said.

"Here, are my keys," she said. "Drive me to look once more,
at the intolerable mystery that is, the Black Forest.
"Well, personally," I muttered, "I should much prefer
to see, your pink canoe-ist (bolt-upright) among the
blonde bush-niche of your succulent thighs." — Ooooo!

Ponsonby

for Jane

What is it with love that it should
    lean over and with a finger
    feather-light, touch your nose
    leading it on to the tip of mine
    in a special kind of kiss — but
    lifting the same finger to warn
    us never to use our noses as
    a pivot for our lips' clamping?

But we have already gone farther
    into a new harbour of our own
    creation: the bumps and hollows
    of our bodies' eloquence nudging,
    an urgent berthing, a classier
    fit? Well, and

    what care we now if love's marae
    formalities desert us; throwing its
    arms up in despair, and in a mock
    bow shew an elegant leg — backing
    out of the room eye-brows raised —
    and quite unnoticed.

A deluge of memory!

I fill my head
    with thoughts
    that are disorderly —
    inordinately so, &
    sexy: for

    you, are not one
    of the human, feeling-
    specie, if, the element
    of sex, is absent from

    your very being, heart,
    lungs, soul, dance-steps —
    & the pistoning-rhythmic
    movement of muscularity
    of the arms, thighs —
    the swank-wank-thwack, of
    hairy gonads, responding
    to the lowered penis-head
    (now, *upraised*) *CHARGE*!!

p.s. is this how you spend your frustrate hours,
Hone? Fine! Stir up a word of thank you for
me, then! *Atua Waiata.*

p.p.s.   Kia Ora!

A brief summation on love

The days pass by
    without let, knowing
    that people can define
    night from day &
    with some inventive
    measure-metre (clock;
    watch) tell midnight
    from mid-day & the
    intervals in between
    for work-sessions,
    rest, & slumber, & daily,
    a renewed interest, from
    time to time — for eat-
    ing, & a cooperative
    activity in working together
    with mates, comrades, &
    with members of one's
    own family; tribe …
    & a concentrated effort

from time to time, to indulge
    in a passionate spasm
    of interest in attracting
    the opposite sex for romantic purposes
    in a warm reciprocal sense of
    mate-ship & lots
    of loving …!!!

pray
       er: to my autumn deity, gosh

when i speak
your name,
gosh

i'm filled
with effulgence
awe, an old pain —
a banked inhibition

that is fire —
with the blinds
drawn over its eyes
as leaves smother

the earth
smelling sharply
of decay — of oils —
biting dryly into
the lungs — and

the lungs whistling
opening out
newly

to lacerate
spears of smoke
lancing them:

o, you plea-
sure me, gosh:
thank
you very mulch

for stooking my sighs and raking
       my breath away like
              like leaves, gosh:
                     like leaves?

Some thoughts on (im)mortality

It is now — November 11th, 2004!

I was born at Kokewai, Mangakahia
  Road, 2¹/₂ miles from the town-
  ship of Kaikohe — just this
  side of our lake, Omapere,
  — and, 3¹/₂ miles eastward
  from Kaikohe, is the healing
  water of the *hot springs*,
      Ngāwha,
      and,
      just
    a quarter mile further
      is a
     smaller
   settlement, & shops,
  a hotel; called Ohaeawai, with
   the Freezing Works,
   another 1¹/₂ miles
     on, at —
    Moerewa —

And, and, just a little further
  on, the site of yet
   another battleground
   with the British
   Soldiery — called
   Rua-peka-peka

    My Birth-date is 21ˢᵗ Oketopa,
     i te Tau hoki, 1922,
     I'm a veteran of
      survival of
     82 years of age
      Oooooo!

Biographical (aged 6–7)

If I may recall, my primary school years, were
   spent in an adequate tin shack, adjacent to a
   market garden in which my father, Ben
   (Peneamine – Benjamin) used two horses to
   pull a single plough-share, to turn the earth
   into earthen furrows to plant a variety of
   vegetable seeds — for a Pākehā owner whose
   antecedents came from Tai Tokerau also (as
   we did) & with whom my Dad & I were
   housed in a leaky corrugated tin shed which
   my Dad repaired adding a wide, open fire,
   corrugated-iron fire-place & chimney, to
   which latter construction, my Dad, Ben, added
   a horizontal pole of steel, from one side of the
   chimney to the other — and from which steel
   hooks were suspended to take the weight of
   tinned vessels for cooking a mixture mostly of
   meats, pūhā, potatoes, marrow & young corn
   (in season) ... with *doughboys*, a Māori form of
   'dumplings'. Oh, Boy! What a succulent
   smorgasbord of KAI!
   O! Yea!!!
   Aghhh ... *Memories*!

Biographical (?)!!! Yes! & devoid of lies!!

The only religious leader
    to whom I bend the knee
    is Saint Fiacre, Patron Saint
    of those who suffer from *haemorrhoids*!

I have to admit, that after 3–4 years working
    at the Otahuhu Railway Workshop (1939–1944), as an
    Apprentice in the noisy & tough Trade of Welder-
    Boilermaker & riveter, I developed an
    ailment which affected me in a painful
    way for many years & which was defined for me, by
    a Railway Doctor, as *bleeding piles*, & which
    was translated for me, as *Haemorrhoids*
    & which affected that area of
    my rectum, which bled profusely. So
    much so, that I was rather careful
    not to leave any sign of blood (aside
    from shit, splattered around the toilet
    'Short Drop' (as distinct from the deep
    pit, and more primitive (and smelly) 'Long
    Drop') with a wooden pole, sited just
    over the edge of a deep hole, & where
    every one came (in their turn) to sit
    on the pole, to grunt & fart & push
    out last night's dinner — or, liquidy
    lunch. And, if your personal plumb-
    ing was in good order — the relief
    had its satisfaction & physical ardour.

Howsome-ever, after a short stay in
Dunedin as the recipient of the literary
'Robert Burns Fellowship' in 1969, and again
in 1974 — and yet again in 1983,
when they offered me a job, sorting out
some historical material, the Hocken
Library had in Collection. I was appointed
Hocken Library Research Fellow — which
I took on with some *trepidation*, as some
of the material dealt with, related
rather, to Ngāi Tahu Genealogical Tables
which I assume were collected by Mr
(or Dr) Hocken — from Ngāi Tahu & other
genealogical descent lines — including the
tribal family of the southernmost parts, to
the Riverton & West Coast of the South Island,
Whaitiri

NO WORRIES — I said a 'protective Māori Chant',
Tai Tokerau origin!!!!

Northcote

In Northcote,
you do not wear one in summer,
because the days
are sunny, kindly & mild.

The Chelsea Sugar Works
weren't that far off
where I used a broom
to sweep the floors clean

The broom handle broke
        in the end,
when I leaned on it, often —

The pay wasn't as heavy
        as a bag of
plucked poultry feathers,
just enough to take home
        to Mum,
for meals and cut lunch.

I love Northcote
and the skies lit up
at night & traffic noises
coming and going
across our harbour bridge;
the mournful sound of
overseas liners, competing with our ferry-boats
for a place to berth — and — and — moonlight

over Rangitoto,
frowning? (No) winking? (No),
well … it's a full moon
going right now;
round and cheezy, & wanting
you to have a big bite,
from his cheezy bum.
Ooooo …!

Refuge at 108 Cannington Road, Māori Hill, Dunedin

To you, house — a house shaped like a square
    horse-shoe (for lucky horsy guys with veiny dorks)

my heart-song deploy
    endowing it with a warm, grainy inlay
    with which the archway of my heart is garlanded
    and which I now bestow unsparingly — coming
    out as if unwilled — sprightly as a spring

    snuckling out of a bank, greenly furnished
    nor lacking the sense and heard eminence of
    grandeur — a voice brushed with a light
    tincture of green, of gold, of silver — and dispensing
    without the noble knob of coarseness hawking
    in the noble throttle of the river's voice.

Thusly, do I choose to thank you house, with
    just a lilt of poetic extravagance to ensparkle
    the dourness of candour and truth. Here, let
    the flora flower florescently, the fauna leap
    fanatically. And I shall smack my lips when
    the dinner-gong goes clack-clack in my belly —
    my voice breaking in a song, thank you …

    And
    to all who enjoy shelter under your rangatira
    roofbeam, together, with mine kind hosts,
    Sue and Richard, and their fine and handsome
    sons, Henry, John, and Ffrederik, my
    haka-call of aroha is clear, emphatic.
    Kia ora koutou — kia ora tātou katoa. Hey!
        I love youse …

Some thoughts on immortality (!)

Something, rather personal, ought to be
    written down, to describe what advances
    have evolved in the humble and
    daily chore of urine & shit disposal
    by the simple act of pressing a button

Oni-orni-thologists — who study the habits
    of the hawking (sometime melodious) and
    'throatie' contribution to other tree-dwellers
    — and — and — who treat me, with circum-
    spection — if not, suspicion & mistrust.

Not to worry (a close enough sound to my very
    own name, Tuwhare! Or, to give it a
    more chieftainly layout (sorry: lay-about)
    on an unmarked surface of writing
    paper! *Hone Tuwhare Peneamine Anatipa
    Te Pona*. Impressed? Well ...)

I mean, who knows? Why, they've already conferred
    upon me, the 'snazzy' title, of *Doctor of Literature* —
    and this, by our *senior* establishment of learning, in
            Aotearoa —
        The University of Otago (wait for it!)
    — on the 12th December, 1998. Y'betcha!!!

On the other hand, my ancestors (& *don't* ask me
    to recite the chiefly lineage. Just accept.)
    I mean, I'm as good as any other professional, in
    trawling-up the bullshit! In this case, though —
    my Ancestors, would consider it an insult if
    I besmirched the human links which tie
        me, indissolubly, to them.

So ... I have a profound respect, to those former
    Ancestral Links of Tree-dwellers.
        A Māori, *Tarzan* of the Ape-man?

Well, I am not being, WHAKA-HI-HI... *No way*...
    or, a big SKITE!!!!

On becoming an Icon (!)

Except for a couple absentee
    Icons, together, we stand —
    all ten of us comically sardonical;
    sartorially
    succeeding only in being
    dark-suited —
    bow-tied & white-shirted,
    but secretly stretched
    in bowel and
    bladder control, as

the Governor-General,
    Dame Silvia pins
    a round, green-stoned-
    cored badge, on our
    plumped-up chests to a series
    of comedically repressed "Ow-ouches"
    and, discovering politically that
    we are all 'Lefties'
    as the pin lances
    a left nipple.

We become more phylosophically
    dead in the face, as
    our lips curl to a
    comedically heroic, tight-
    lipped silence of
    painful acceptance,
    laconically iconical!

Time is my blue & red tea-pot

You're not a friend, but a compulsive
    companion of my Old Age, Time.
    I define you only as the space
    between my last meal and the next.
    In between meals, you force me to
    defecate on you; pass water, and
    other normal human functions.

You hang around and about me for no
    other reason than a vague gesture
    a promise, that you are a part of
    me — and as personal to me as my
    blue and red Tea-pot — and my dog
    HIKI, who identifies me as a kind
    and generous fixture with a smell
    that is not alien or threatening.

I pursue you, Time, but I cannot catch
    up with you, so I think I will switch
    the electric jug on and jam my blue
    and red Tea-pot on top of it to heat
    up, before I chuck a half a palm of
    tea-leaves in it — to warm.

I'm engulphed by you, Time, though not
    as completely as you've already done
    to some loved friends. They precede
    me like the echo of sad footfalls in
    my heart ... fading away. As of now,
    tears pool my eyes. I turn back to
    seek a solace in a frenzied search
    for my beginnings: my Self.

My empty, unwashed, blue and red Tea-pot
    stares me down in reproach. I wash it
    inside and out, switch the hot water
    jug on, grab a handful of biscuits and
    open the door. HIKI is right there —
    coy and wiggly.

Where the flaming *hell* are ya, Māori man?

Inflammably, the fire, in my Wagener
   cast-iron stove catches on — with
   a cheekful of blown air, expelled
   towards the base of a lit-up heap
   of kindling-wood, to help it along …
The flame now, to my delight, has caught
   on, and has adopted a senior role —
   in a Supervisionary sense of Referee-ship,
   to adjudge the crackle-bite, & sound
   of wood, the fire rebelliously & incontestably alive,
   and to the fore!

It is disclaiming in a forceful orangie-
   coloured voice, "Feed me! Feed me!
   Ya laid-back Māori man — Come on!
   Move it! Get off that cozy twin-armed
   chair — and, arm yourself, with a lethal,
   newly-filed axe-blade! I want to see
   and hear — the swing and whirl, of
   the Sun-trapped axe-blade, biting
   deep into the heavy chunks of wood."
   I can still feel & hear, my Wagener stove-mouth
   complaining harshly… instructively —
      FEED ME, YA MĀORI BUGGAR!
      GET OFF YOUR ARSE! LET
      ME SEE AND HEAR THE SWING
      AND THE BITE OF THE
         AXE-BLADE ON WOOD-
         CHUNKS … HUGE,
         AND, LONG OF LENGTH,
         LIKE MY MĀORI
         COCK!
      (just joking… just choking)

Yes! And let me feel the axe-blade
   clumping & chomping into the wood …
   MOVE IT, MAN … GO FOR IT!

Well … (thoughts on one's immortality?!) by a socialist-minded rebel & Marxist

It's not
another, intellectual paean
of pain —
but one worked diligently at
to disguise its
ugly format — the
huge stone archway of crumbling chips
of rocks quarried long-since
by poor subject black
slaves
forced
to work for a Slave Master
(& later still — a Feudal
Lord) — useless
bloody blood-sucking
Masters of Property &
a Minority Money-Class
— with immense
accumulated riches
of landed Estates, factories,
Coal Mines (not to
speak of Diamond ones)
Property &
the constant twist & soulless,
non-think exertion to squeeze
the last pint of drying sweat from
the muscle and brow of his
team of slave-labour —
from
whose labour-power the Capitalist
exploiter builds and builds and builds
— a vast accumulated Capital to be
re-invested — in buying more, cheaper-costing
slaves (black-skinned), these
times & *plentiful*!

'I feel like a vulnerable pā-site'

I feel like a vulnerable
    pā-site, sacked, by
    an unforgiving enemy
    force & razed to a level
    unbecoming, to a warrior-force,
    but — freed at last,
    to accept — with humility —
    the earth-smelling pungency
    of that Grand Dame — mother,
    of us all: Papa-tū-ā-Nuku:
    our Earth-mum.

A 'piss-up' pome!

I'm reminded of the Beatle song group —
who lament questionably: who is
gonna feed one, when ya reach
the age of Sixty-four (64) But...

at a riper age of Eighty-two (82)
I have a problem of defining who
really is the Boss — excluding, that
is, the Top Dog (the Pot God) living
high, high up, in the Top Floor, of
the multi-storied Tower! Well ...

I mean, let me state the bare facts — because
it is all of that, & more! Well...
The bulbous pomposity of my penis-
head, isn't really the bossy Overseer
that *it* makes out to be. Because,
every time I need (with some urgency
I might add) to direct my 'Urine
Exit Stem' & directly target the
middle of the white porcelain bowl,
what does it, do? Well ...

I mean, well ...
The jet stream of urine, multiplies
instead, *into three* (!) infamous
jet-streams of piss! The infamy
of it all!!! It tries to be
strictly, '*democratic*', & despite my
lamentable effort at control, my left
pants-leg is wettened, as is my
right pants-leg! And the middle
jet at least, smears the forward
rim, of the Classical shape
of the modern, '*Short-drop*'(!!!)

I sigh despairingly at this kind of
   'knobbly' (not at all, NOBLE) per-
   versity! It does mean, that —
   more scrubbing & laundering of trousers!
   It reminds me that a spare pair of trousers
   is drying on the clothes-line, & which needs
   to be unpegged & brought in before
   rainy-clouds, give it an extra rinsing. From
   this personal discourse, you may gain some
   understanding that when you're 82 years
   of age (as my Gods decree) my bladder
   storage capacity is somehow reduced.
   An 'outstanding' problem, rather!!!

Who are you?

If I were rangatira
    (a very minor one)
    I'd make a deeper
    wish to even be
    more humble than
    I can ever be
    so that no
    official impedi-
    ment may get
    in the way
    of my being
    fully & consciously
    aware that being
    humble; is as
    natural as trees waving
    birds singing: sun shining …

Restorative work on ... 'humility'. Aa-e, hoki!

I am sick
   of listening to a boring 'recitative'
   of all the qualities that I may fulsomely
   qualify — for the Kiwi commonplace,
   of "Good on ya, Mate... Take
   a step-up the ladder of Fame (!)"
But you've already achieved
     the un-achievable, by having
conferred upon you (by the grace &
recommendation of an un-identifiable
Selection Panel of Six, 'academics', whose
names were never revealed,
        publicly (!) Or, to me!!

So... (and, so?) I have the distinct-
   ion of wearing the label — if I need
   it — as, 'Doctor of Literature'. An
Academic Distinction, I push aside
& would, *personally not — in any way*
pick up voluntarily & affix to my
signature, trumpeting, so that the WORLD
     (I mean, THE 'WHOLE' WORLD!!!)
should know, that I am embarrassingly
   stuck with something un-alluringly
      meaningless. '*Pono...*'
THAT ... pushed aside (and by me, forgotten)
   I pack away an un-sharpened pencil,
     an inkless pen (!)
   Humbly, I turn instead, to my
   ancestral connections to give
'em, two stiff, upraised fingers of independent
humility — and acquiescence, together, with, the
secret joy of, *BELONGING* & being *possessed*.
'Kia Ora, koutou, e ōku nei Tūpuna... Ara,
Tātou katoa!
Aaa-e, maarika hoki ... YES!   87

A short 'ditty' for my 82nd birthday!
The poem: 'Rail stop, & refreshments'(!)

Dreams,
    never coyly front-up,
    permissively or, if you may
    allow — admissively … Er, wot
    doy ya reckon!?

Wal … Wot do I reckon?
    It's a hard one. The Consultation Hours,
    for a sympathetic hearing
    one hopes — and, con-
    jointly, that is — with, my Unconscious
    — is rather difficult to arrange
    for some Specific Meeting-time
    you see …?

Howsome-ever (wot a boon —
    long words, in English are!)
    That clumsy length of English
    'atrocity', however, rhymes
    rather well (I consider,
    sagely) with: … and … and —

just after the pinkishly-alert
    guardian — that we may call the
    Woman's Holy Clitorium (paid holy-homage to
    by many tongues — 'saliva-lilly'
    awash, with anticipatory sounds of:
      "Lickety-licky" — Yummy-yum!)
        Oooooo …

Wal, ya know — I have the 'mileage'
    — and, could, forever —
    go on & on & on — WHOA!
    But — but — but … I,
    will refrain —
    if only to take a very short 'break',
    to prepare some energy-building
    'Kai' — for my love & I …

Just drifting ... Hone

When light from the Moon
    falls on the corrugated
    roof of my Long Drop —
    I say to my self (and, askance-
    ly, & thankfully, to that Great
    Fellow Up Above), WOT
    a fortunate Fella I am to
    have a Speedway track
    to my Shit House, so that
    the troublesome internal
    waste-product may be
    unceremoniously unburdened
    thusly, making more room
    for the next load of waste
    product to build satisfac-
    tory in systematic
    heaps for sorting — so that
    the vitamints from each food-
    source, contribute to the
    necessity of adding mile-age
    to a life-time of snoring &
    waking up to eat, to shit,
    and to not only smack the
    cheeks of me bum, my
    Māori chops — my Pisser!
      Ooooooo ... ooo!

To Hine-nui-te-Pō — the fat bitch!

Now if —
    (a big — big, 'if') I were
    a Rangatira, O, boy!
    Wot tribute-paying tribes
    would I command
    to kneel before the elegant
    taiaha of your succulent
    beauty — and, and ... to swear

    allegiance, to your lips
    your saucy eyes, yr rhythmic
    hips & bum ... *Oooooo!*

O, yes! beneath yr big flat feet
    what jewels I would fling!
    The stars shall be yr pearls —
    actually fragmented purple pāua-shells,
    the World —
    The World?? O!! Yes — yes!!

The World: shall be a huge black oyster-
    pearls on a muka flax-string — and YOU
    shall have orange-tinted clouds to wear
    at Sunrise (for decorative purposes. Er, strictly)
    if, I were
    a Rangatira!

Let me rest my head on your fat belly, hine feel/sniff you up — ooops!

I don't know if my dreams are slyly usurping my
startled/wide-awake thoughts, as there are
no clear lines or division between them.
I cluck, like a bird, a hen — fart, roll over
on my left side — my right (without any fear
of losing my political orientation) coaxingly
inviting the Queen of Sleep to empower my
snores to a remarkable level of pitch, a
stumbling staccato of ecstatic grossness — I,
have already recorded, in my Diary, caustic
comments about my nasal contribution, by three
distraught female companions, post coitus-ically
speaking (at different times; naturally) And now
there are motorized-sounds, as I drift off — I,
am a chugging motor-boat in a dark Sea of in-
comprehension and resignation, as I lollop-off to
mine own Sleep-den of thankful rest & oblivion.

Hmmmm ...

It is a house which requires
    care in construction.

It has no walls thus permitting
    expansion. The ceiling
    is unlimited stretching to heaven.

It may endure given a chance
    that's for sure: hmmmm ...

Because it is of earth, smelling
    of earth, its foundation
    may be built on sand.

It may be a house built on thin
    wooden legs, steadfast, and
    walking into a river swollen
    suddenly by a cloud-burst;
    or, a house-boat chundered-out
    and abandoned on a reef of mud.

But since there are no walls — or roof
    to it, love may be seen as bars
    of feeling — tones and colour, warm
    cold, hot, grey and with lots
    of blue, or just plain
    shitty coloured!

Fleshed out though, the house of love
    isn't shapeless. It has presence.
    It has form — a brilliant arc
    uniting heaven and earth: actually
    love-thoughts seeking a new way
    of expression: aha, aha aha
    as horses pounding into the straight
    riders snarling — the anguish
    of stretched leather smelling of sweat.

If I should die, think nothing (nihil) of it.
Happens, naturally ... to all.

To my deaf ear, I raise
    the Wrist to which
    my watch is strapped
    just barely noting
    the tiniest intervals
    between the tick and
    tock of it, inexorably
    paging — unemotionally
    and without the least
    evidence of compassionate
    interest the leaching, leaking
    moments between your
    arrival, and final nod-off
    &... goodbyes — of your
    departure time:
    One last emptying of the bowel
    and piss-bag: tick-tick
    tock, hands off cock —
    er ... tick ... tick ... tick.
    O, excelsior! Full marks!
    Mayhap, your great, great
    grandnephews, nieces, will inherit
    your wrist-watch
    & reclaim, the rhythm
    the 4/4 Boogie beat of your heart.
    For, on their tiny feet
    you march.

To Elespie, Ian & their Holy Whānau

On life's eternal river
    we float on … and
    on, forever — like
    a stream of light
    enhancing our under-
    standing of human love,
    and life! Kia ora!

Dr Ian Prior
96 Wade Street
Wellington

To Elespie, Ian & their
Holy Whanau — from Hone
On Life's eternal River
we float on … and
on, forever — like
a stream of light
enhancing our under-
standing of human Love,
and Life! Kia Ora!
Hone

NOTES

p12 Hone says "ten (10)", but he's actually published 13 previous books, many with multiple editions.

p20 Blackwood & Janet Paul Ltd published *No Ordinary Sun* in 1964. Janet Paul was made Dame Companion of the New Zealand Order of Merit in 1997 for services to the arts; she died in 2003.

p21-34 Kereihi, Hone's close friend Shirley Grace McGregor (born 1949) was an actor (*Goodbye Pork Pie* and other films), photographer, painter and film-maker. She lived at Tomarata/Pakiri and died in 2000 of breast cancer.

p25 The return of the swallows to the old mission at Capistrano, California, is celebrated by an annual fiesta and in a famous song.

p52 This poem and p76 'Northcote' have been transcribed from poems written for Northcote Primary School, courtesy of Susan Woods.

p64, 65: Lady Fiona Elworthy, close friend.

p74 Saint Fiacre, a hermit with the gift of healing, is patron saint of barrenness, gardening, cab drivers ... and haemorrhoids.

p77 Richard & Sue Hatherly and their sons Henry, John, and Frederick are long-term Dunedin friends.

p78 *Oni-orni-thologists:* onioni is a Māori term for having sex.

p79 In 2003 the Arts Foundation of New Zealand honoured Hone as one of its first ten Icon Artists.

p80 Elements of this poem appear in the much briefer 'Time out', *Shape-Shifter* 1997.

p94 Ian and Elespie Prior are old friends; Elespie died in 2002.

Various poems: Louis Armstrong, Coleman Hawkins, Gene Krupa, Thelonius Monk and Artie Shaw are all renowned U.S. blues or jazz musicians.

CD: *tuwhare*

Released May 2005:
a selection of Hone's
poems set to contem-
porary original music
and performed by some
of Aotearoa NZ's top musicians: Hinemoana Baker,
Jonathan Besser, Whirimako Black, Graham Brazier,
Goldenhorse, Dean Hapeta/Te Kupu, Hone Hurihanganui,
Don McGlashan, strawpeople, Dallas Tamaira,
Mahinarangi Tocker, WAI (Mina Ripia & Maaka Phat)
and Charlotte Yates.

Available from good music stores

DVD: *Hone Tuwhare ~ The Return Home*

Coming soon in 2005 on DVD is Michele McGregor's
documentary of Hone's tour of Te Tai Tokerau (Northland)
with poet Glenn Colquhoun, guitarist Nopera Pikari and
singer Mahina Kaui. The DVD includes the full-length
version of the film, extra poems and conversations, the full
version of Hone's talk to writing students, and interview and
incidental footage.

For more information, contact: info@steeleroberts.co.nz
or Michele: info@bluetotara.com ~ www.bluetotara.com

---

www.HoneTuwhare.co.nz

Launching in July 2005 ~ the official website, featuring
biographical notes, poems, bibliography, products
and Hone Tuwhare news and information.